HOW TO PASS IT ON:

THE OWNERSHIP AND USE OF SUMMER HOUSES

KEN HUGGINS

and

JUDITH HUGGINS BALFE

ISBN Number 1-57087-488-3
Library of Congress Catalog Number 99-093343

Pocomo Press
Montclair, NJ 07043

Manufactured in the United States of America
00 01 02 03 10 9 8 7 6 5 4 3 2

HOW TO PASS IT ON:
THE OWNERSHIP AND USE OF SUMMER HOUSES

Ken Huggins and Judith Huggins Balfe

CONTENTS

HOW TO PASS IT ON:
THE OWNERSHIP AND USE OF SUMMER HOUSES

INTRODUCTION

We are brother and sister who have vacationed on our family property in Nantucket Island, Massachusetts for forty years. Our father, who died in 1985, bought the land and built the two houses our family members occupy during the summer. "Our family" once meant another brother and sister and our parents -- and other relatives whom we seldom saw. It now includes our individual nuclear families, as all four of us are married and have two children apiece; our older brother has five grandchildren. So for us, "our family" now includes in-laws, nieces and nephews, and even grand-nieces and nephews. It also includes a couple of ex-spouses, who are part of our collective memories of our summer houses.

Despite our father's careful estate planning, designed to keep our summer houses in the family, since our mother's death in 1997 we have all been dealing with unresolved questions of our inheritance: the allocation and scheduling of summer "slots;" paying for maintenance, taxes, and capital improvements; figuring out how our children will get some time of their own there during the summer; arranging and paying for the opening and closing of the houses; and so on and so forth, et cetera, ad infinitum, and sometimes, ad nauseam.

Over the span of years that we have enjoyed our summer home, we have encountered many families with similar places, and heard many horror stories of families at odds, in conflict, even torn forever asunder by the difficulties of resolving the differences. This hasn't happened to us, but we have had our share of difficulties. Having a natural interest in the subject, Judy, with a Ph.D. in Sociology and a position as professor of sociology at the College of Staten Island-City University of New

York, searched the sociological literature to find out what researchers and scholars have learned about inheritance and use of summer homes. She discovered that no one has even looked into the subject. There is nothing published on what enables an extended family to manage and use a summer house, to be emulated — let alone on what leads instead to family disintegration over the sale of the house, to be avoided. This, then, was the impetus for Judy's scholarly study of such practices: *Passing It On: The Inheritance and Use of Summer Houses.* It is being published simultaneously with this briefer and more light-hearted workbook version derived from her findings.

Ken has an Ed.D., has done a wide range of educational research, and currently teaches English at Monroe Community College in Rochester, N.Y. He is primary author of this version of the story. It is written for members of families with summer houses who want guidance in specific ways to resolve differences, make decisions on maintenance and usage, and draft formal agreements which could preclude the kind of horror stories we have heard too much about, but who may be less interested in the serious sociological analysis found in Judy's nearly 300-page book.

Together, we assume that if you are reading this, you now have a summer house, alone or with other family members, or are contemplating owning one. You may instead have a ski lodge, an alternative type of vacation home. If you intend that to be passed on to your heirs, the same issues will arise. Whatever the family property and your interest in this book, we intend it to be informational, raising specific questions for you to address. As you read along, we suggest that you jot down notes, memories, issues, ideas, etc. which may be useful to you as you work toward resolving your own issues (and there are *always* issues!) concerning your vacation property, leading to the development of a formal agreement with your heirs or co-owners. If other members of your family are interested in joining you in this inquiry, you might all get copies of the book and make notes for comparative purposes.

Naturally, we think this is a wonderful idea. Even better, buy one copy of Judy's book to serve as basic reference source and many copies of this one, so that even the less scholarly family members can participate knowledgeably in the discussion.

All specific places, families, individuals described in this book are fictional. All situations and family dynamics are amalgams of real and invented elements. If you see yourself or your family in anything we describe, it simply means that there are many other people in situations like yours, who have collectively served as the basis of the scenarios we present here.

In anticipation of these scenarios, sketch out a family tree below, including all with some claim to your summer house or other vacation property, starting with the "founders," be they yourselves, your parents or grandparents. Figure 1 ("the Madisons" and Figure 2 ("the Murphys") below can give you useful models for your sketch. Making it will help you keep in mind all of those whose various interests need to be considered if you are to successfully pass on the ownership and use of your place.

CHAPTER 1
TWO TYPICAL FAMILY SCENARIOS

While the families and family houses Judy has studied are so diverse as to preclude identifying any single "typical" situation, the two extended families described below embody many of the issues and dynamics commonly found in the subject of her study. They are described in some detail because only through such detail can one illustrate the range and complexity of summer house use. It is likely that certain details will resonate with you; at least we hope so. We want an emotional reaction to what we describe, not just an intellectual one. We are sure that you have strong feelings about your summer house, and it is these feelings, properly channeled, that will lead to make the best decisions about this use for you, your offspring, and subsequent generations.

In the midst of and at the end of each of the following scenarios, we have left space for you to record some notes about your family, some comparisons and contrasts you see with "the Madisons" and "the Murphys." The Madisons are dealing with the transition of authority and ownership of their summer house from the "founders" to their children, the second generation. The Murphys are dealing with an even more complex transition from the second generation to the third.

After you have taken some notes, we would recommend that you then write the story of your own family and summer house in the manner we have illustrated. If you find writing difficult because of chronic writer's cramp, lack of paper, or glitches in your electronic whatsis, try dictating into a tape recorder. Even better, have other family members do the same, and then compare versions. Note that we have made a strong attempt to be objective and unbiased in these descriptions. This was easy for us here, since these particular families are fictional, and not our own. (Our family appears in various disguises in Judy's book, but not here.) It may be hard for you to be objective, but you aren't publishing your own story (yet), so work at it.

THE MADISONS

The Madison family owns a three-bedroom cottage on two acres of waterfront property on Cape Cod, Massachusetts. Carlton Madison, the founder, bought the land and built the cottage in the early 1960s, which he named "Whispering Grasses." He has been dead for eight years. Ginger, his widow, is now 78 and lives year round in the Albany, NY area. She likes to spend four to five weeks each summer at the summer house, while one or another of her children is in residence there with their families. She is proud to be the matriarch of the family and loves to talk about her four children, their spouses, and her seven grandchildren. As issues have developed and some conflicts surfaced, she has encouraged her children: "Talk it out, just truly listen to each other with love in your hearts." She dismissed a recent suggestion that it might be a good idea to develop a written, formal agreement as to use and maintenance of "Whispering Grasses." The idea of any structured legal agreement, an association or corporation, is anathema to her, as it would seem to violate the principle of shared love among all family members to which she has devoted her life..

Ginger has been able to maintain this view in part because Carlton established a trust fund to cover taxes and maintenance of their place, so she hasn't had to worry much about how to pay for it. However, taxes and expenses have increased for more rapidly than expected, and currently, there is a $6-7,000 shortfall which the family must make up. It is likely that this shortfall will increase. As is often the case with trusts, the Madison trust says nothing about how the places is to be used, who gets which weeks, how repairs are to be handled, etc. What is clear and fully understood is that when Ginger dies, her four children will inherit her estate, including Whispering Grasses, in equal measures. These four, their spouses, and their children are as follows, in order of birth:

Thomas, a successful lawyer, is married to Stacy, a homemaker. They have four children, and live in the Boston area. Doug and his wife Gwen are both social workers. They have two children, and live in New Jersey. Silvia and her husband,

Fig.1 THE MADISON FAMILY TREE

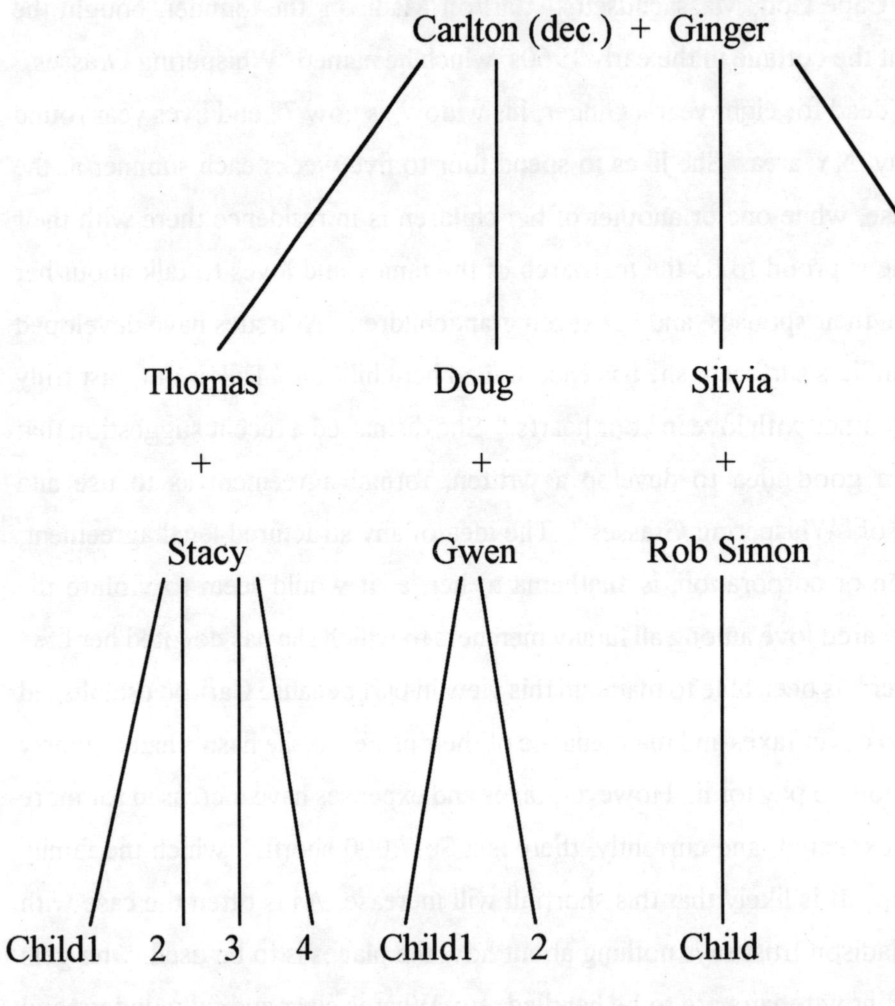

Rob are both skilled craft makers, living in Mystic, Connecticut with their intentionally only child. Fred, the youngest, lives in the Chicago area with his wife Karen. He has a small advertising agency and she is a buyer for a department store. They are deliberately childless.

The four Madison offspring divide up the nine prime summer months of July and August into specific two and a half week slots. They schedule these with Ginger, rotating first, second, third choice on a yearly basis so that she can visit with at least three of them during her own mid-summer visits. They sometimes negotiate swaps of slots and choices depending on their children's summer schedules and individual preferences for times. These negotiations are not easy and there has been some tension around them, especially as they go through Ginger.

Because of their distance from Cape Cod, Fred and Karen come east just once every three years. When they do, they get first choice for a slot. When they don't, the families of Thomas, Doug and Silvia could each have a little more than three weeks. However, Doug and Karen, and sometimes Silvia and Rob, can't take more than two to two and a half weeks. So there have been days, occasionally even a week, when the place is not used. This has been a source of some frustration but Doug and Silvia are unwilling just to give Thomas their extra days without some compensation.

The new and increasing shortfall from the trust fund is now being made up equally by the four siblings, as was stipulated in Carlton's will. The outlay has been no problem for Thomas and Fred, but it is something of a difficulty for Doug, and a real problem for Silvia. Thomas has said that he is willing to pay all the expenses, but in return for that, he wants three full weeks each summer and first choice of slots every year. So far, the others haven't agreed.

Other issues have surfaced and are causing increasing tension and conflict. None have been resolved and they are threatening the peace and solidarity of the Madison family. These issues include the following:

Thomas wants to add another bedroom and bath to the cottage since with four children, his family is quite crowded. He would like to take on a home improvement loan, with all sharing the costs, but as with his suggestion on expenses, he has gotten no agreement. He could afford to build the addition himself, but is reluctant to do so and let the others "freeload" on his generosity. He points out that he has replaced appliances and furniture without asking for any compensation.

Thomas is the only one of the four with the time and resources to come down to the Cape for a few days in June or September. Doug and Silvia feel that because he can do this, he should not get a crack at first choice in the prime months.

Further, Thomas's firstborn child, Carl, was married two years ago and his first grandchild, Ginger's first great-grandchild, is expected in a few months. Carl has mentioned that he would like a summer slot of his own, which has taken Thomas' three siblings by surprise.

Of Ginger's four children, Doug is the closest to her emotionally. Ginger is also very fond of his wife Gwen, who has similar tastes to her own, as her daughter, Silvia, does not. So Ginger prefers to come to the Cape for all of Doug's slot, spending a few days with whoever precedes and follows him. Doug is willing to allow this, but he is beginning to resent the fact that he and Gwen never have the place to themselves. They have never been able to invite guests to share their slot, as his siblings do.

Silvia and Rob enjoy working on the cottage and land and are acknowledged to have put far more "sweat equity" into Whispering Grasses than anyone else. They have made a number of repairs which have saved a good deal of money, given the cost of hiring local service people. These two are sailors and recently purchased a small sailboat. Given the relative fragility of the sailboat and the trickiness of local winds, they have asked that no one else use it, though it remains on the property when they are not there. This is the first instance of a piece of property being other than family owned.

Thomas is resentful of this, since he has guests who come down every year, staying in a nearby motel, who are experienced sailors and he would like to have them be able to use the boat. Fred and Karen have done some sailing on Lake Michigan and would like to try saltwater sailing as well, and they are miffed that Silvia and Rob are adamant that no one else uses their boat.

Silvia is frustrated with her mother's conservative tastes and would like to spruce up the cottage. On her own, she threw out the old drapes for the living room picture window and made new ones of much brighter colors. No one else likes the new drapes and angry words have been exchanged over the imperious way in which she made the change. Since she is the only daughter, she feels that it is her right to eventually assume her mother's role as arbiter of decisions about furnishings and décor. However, Ginger usually first talks about such matters to her daughters-in-law, Stacy and Gwen, and is influenced far more by them, especially as Thomas has paid for most of the changes. This adds further to Silvia's resentments.

Spending two out of every three summers around the Great Lakes, Fred and Karen find themselves drawing emotionally away from Whispering Grasses. Having no children to spend summers there, Fred finds that his ties to the place have diminished over time, and he has no reason to pressure Karen to strengthen her own. In addition, as Fred is five years younger than Silvia, his closest sibling, he has never felt that he is fully equal to her — let alone to their older brothers. He is getting tired of the increasing bickering and quarreling over some of these issues concerning the sharing of the summer house. He and Karen have thought about reserving their slot each year but then renting it for the two years they don't come. Knowing how ticklish this might be, Fred hasn't raised the question with his siblings, but he would like to do so.

Indeed, Fred has mentioned a couple of times to Thomas that after Ginger dies, he might like to be bought out of his share of the property. The latter, who by age and profession has naturally taken over the financial and legal paperwork of the property, has not mentioned this to the others. He knows that Doug and Silvia would be unable to contribute to a buyout. He might be able to handle this himself, but he also knows that if he then owned half of the property, with Doug and Silvia each owning a quarter, there would be an even greater number of problems.

One other thing Thomas is aware of is that the Commonwealth of Massachusetts will hit them very hard on the inheritance of a summer house, as it is all still in Ginger's name. It is even possible that the place would have to be sold just to pay the inheritance taxes. He has talked with Ginger about considering ways to give the property to the children before she dies, but she seems incapable or unwilling to understand his reasoning.

Finally, the winds and salt air are tough on Cape Cod houses. Whispering Grasses desperately needs a new roof and a new coat of paint on the extensive trim that sets off the unpainted shingles. Local estimates for this are in the $7-8,000 range. Silvia and Rob are willing the do these jobs if the others pay for materials and they get three full weeks and first choice for slots for three years. Though very skilled in a variety of craftwork, neither has done any roofing and their painting has been limited to interiors. The matter is under discussion.

Here then, are the questions the Madison family is trying to resolve. Space has been left for you to make any notes that occur to you, should you see these questions as relevant to your own situation.

Should Ginger remain in charge of scheduling?

Is there an easier way to negotiate swapping slots?

Should Fred and Karen get first choice every third year if the others then get first choice less often?

Who could or should use the place if there are periods when no family member is present?

If Thomas assumes a greater burden of the expenses, which he is better able to do, should he be compensated with extra time or more frequent first choice of dates?

Considering the prospect of grandchildren, should Whispering Grasses be enlarged? Is so, who should pay for this?

If Thomas comes down in June and September, should he still be able to take a normal July and August slot?

Should Thomas's son, Carl, be allowed to choose a slot of his own, or should he negotiate with his father for part of his time? As Carl's siblings and cousins get older and start their families, how can everyone get some time at Whispering Grasses?

Should Ginger rotate whom she stays with? If she continues to always stay more with Doug, should he receive some compensation?

What is Silvia and Rob's "sweat equity" worth? Does it entitle them to anything? For that matter, the others do put in some sweat equity of their own; how can they determine how much each has done and what should it be worth?

Should any of the siblings be allowed to maintain personal property at Whispering Grasses that the others cannot use?

Should Silvia take over her mother's role vis-à-vis décor and furnishings? Or should this be assumed by her and all the daughters-in-law together? If Thomas assumes more of the costs, should this role then devolve to Stacy? Come to think of it, should this be exclusively a "women's" role?

Should Fred and Karen be allowed to take their slot and rent it? If so, to whom? And where should the rental money go? Since they are in Chicago, who would act as landlord, making sure the place is ready for occupancy, collecting rental, etc.?

If Fred and Karen ever do want to sell out their share, how should this be handled? What plans could be made now to deal with it later?

What can they do now to avoid the heavy inheritance taxes likely to fall on them at Ginger's death?

Who should paint and roof the house, and how should it be paid for?

The Madison siblings have been trying to deal with these issues following Ginger's dictum to "talk it out, listen with love in your hearts," but it's not working. Tension, conflict, and confrontation increase, especially as it is nearly impossible for them all to get together face-to-face to discuss the matter collectively. When they do meet, usually just two of the couples together, old wounds from earlier sibling rivalries are reopened, and blood and bile rise accordingly. All of them are angry, for different reasons, and scared that they may not be able to hold together as a family. Some, or all, could lose their precious hold on Whispering Grasses, and this is even more frightening. Meanwhile, Ginger shows signs of stress and depression. She doesn't understand why they can't all get along better, and she is very frustrated that she can do nothing to help.

Does this family need to work out a formal agreement, dealing with the current issues and anticipating future ones? We wouldn't be writing this book if we didn't think the answer was a strong "yes." The Madisons are not unusual in the difficulties they are having. In fact, they are handling them better than many families we are aware of, in that they are discussing them openly. Yet the issues that they are dealing with are not going to go away by themselves, and as the next generation grows, more issues will arise. We know of summer houses that are currently being occupied by the fifth and sixth generations. Just consider what happens when a family gets to be that large, with many members who may want a piece of the summer while others want to be bought out. Without some kind of formal agreement designed to deal with the specific issues such an extended family will face, collective ownership would be impossible!

NOTES – In the above, what resonates or rings a bell about your own situation?

THE MURPHYS

The now deceased founders, George and Frieda Murphy, built a three bedroom log cabin, “Pine Haven,” on five acres of land in the Allegheny Mountains of Pennsylvania in the late 1930s. The wooded land is beautiful and there is a lovely trout stream meandering through their property. There is a large living room with dining area, and huge working fireplace; the eat-in kitchen completes the downstairs. Upstairs are the three bedrooms and a full bath. As their three children, George Jr., Philip and Rose started families, the Murphys attached a large shed-roofed addition to the back of the cabin. Up to six children can sleep there, dormitory fashion, in rather spartan accommodations. There is a half bath in one corner of the addition.

Over the years, the Murphy clan has developed what we would call “Informal Complex Ownership” of Pine Haven. There is a semi-formal structure for finances and use, but what really determines how things are run is tradition. All the children and most of the grandchildren remember how George Sr. and Frieda did things — and they try to carry on in those tradition.

George Jr. has inherited from his father the oversight of details regarding Pine Haven. He handles all paperwork and has arranged the summer schedule with his late brother, Philip, and sister, Rose. Philip and Rose were happy to let him do this, and there were few problems among the three in their cooperative use of Pine Haven until Rose divorced Stan Porter when her son Will was small, and married Jim Pearson, a divorcee with a daughter of his own; they have since had two children together.

George Jr. usually hosts a large family gathering right after Christmas at his home near Philadelphia. It has always been expected that all the Murphy clan would attend, no matter what the distance. At this gathering, problems occurring at Pine Haven have been discussed, and assessments of expenses have been made. But as the clan has grown, some of the third generation has started to resent the necessity of coming to George Jr.'s. Some have to travel quite a distance and stay in motels, as his house has just two extra bedrooms. “The cousins,” as they are known, also feel

Fig.2

MURPHY FAMILY TREE

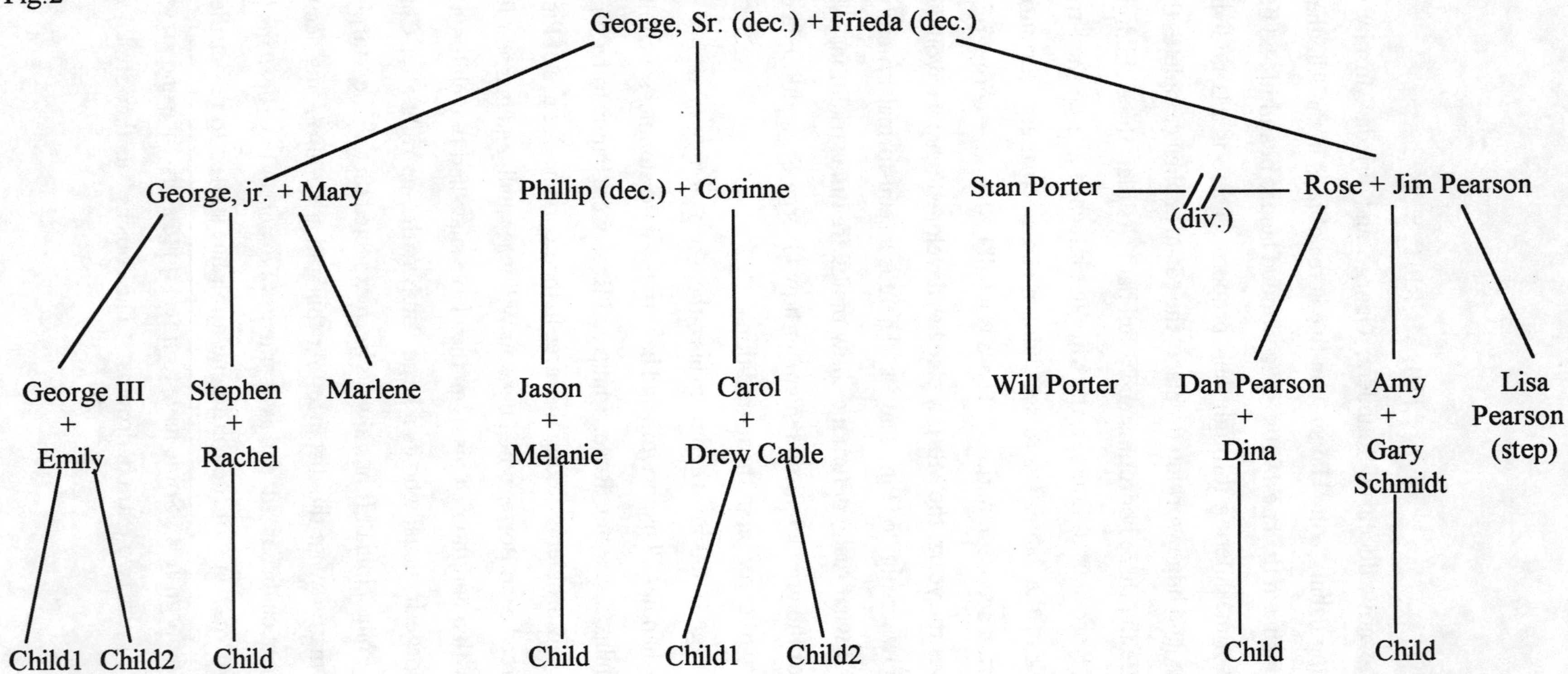

None of the fourth generation is older than 8

that since they have had little say in decisions, their presence should not be required.

George Sr. and Frieda died within a short time of each other, willing Pine Haven to their three children equally and with no inheritance tax due, given its primitive character and low assessment at the time. As they were all in comparatively comfortable financial circumstances, George, Philip, and Rose faced few of the difficulties presented by the Madisons, whose scenario we have just considered. The siblings and their families happily divided July and August into three week slots, and as it turned out, would usually take the same ones. After Philip's untimely death to cancer, his widow Corinne has been granted what are essentially "partner's" rights. George, Philip and Rose always divided expenses equally, and since Corinne has partner's rights, she is expected to pay for her third. However, as Philip's pension and Social Security benefits have not fully compensated for his now lost income, this has been difficult for her to manage. Her children, Jason and Carol, have helped her out, to the extent that they now pay two thirds of her share, together about 22% of the overall expenses.

The Murphy sons' families and thus their children have always been closer to each other than to their Porter/Pearson cousins. It is complicated enough with Will Porter, their same-age first cousin, with whom they have less in common than with each other. Relations with Rose's children — Porter and Pearsons alike — are compounded by the fact that their Pearson step-cousin, Lisa, has come to Pine Haven with her father and stepmother Rose and loves the place. She would like to be considered on an equal plane with the other cousins, but they do not think of her that way.

Under the lead of the Murphy cousins, the eight consanguinary cousins (excluding Lisa) have discussed the current arrangements and they don't like the fact that they must negotiate with their parents for time at Pine Haven. This is especially irksome to Jason Murphy and Carol Cable, since they pay so much of the expenses, as well as to George Murphy, III, oldest of them all. Three years ago, the eight met and drafted a proposal to their parents. Their suggestion was that the eight cousins and their three sets of parents be considered on equal terms, making eleven "units" eligible for summer slots. They further proposed that the summer be considered as including the first week of September, so that there would be eleven weeks of summer. Then each unit would draw straws for a selection position, after which, choice would be rotated, first chooser going to eleventh and the others moving up one. Swapping or even sale of choices among units would be permitted, but not position of choice. One unit could also agree to share with another unit, so that it would be possible that individuals could spend two, or even three weeks at Pine Haven. In addition, expenses would be divided by eleven and that figure would be the weekly user fee.

George, Jr., Philip's widow Corinne, and Rose and Jim listened to this idea, thought about it, and have rejected it. They feel the current procedure is fine. Naturally, this has caused some animosity in the third generation toward their parents. George III, a successful accountant, is particularly angry with his father, who, he feels, has never given him credit for being a mature adult. His cousins Jason Murphy and Carol Cable are also very angry since they are already paying expenses. Finally, Will Porter, Dan Pearson and Amy Schmidt are very upset — but with Jim Pearson. They feel that their mother, Rose, was willing to make the change, but that Jim's influence caused her to vote against it.

Jim's ability to influence Rose may be partly due to the fact that she is demonstrating early signs of Alzheimer's Disease. Though just 62, she is getting forgetful, confused about who is who in the family, and is subject to abrupt mood swings. Her mother Frieda died of Alzheimer's so there is a strong probability that these symptoms are indeed of that disease. This concerns everyone in the family. Since Corinne inherited partner's rights on Philip's death, there is precedent for Jim Pearson claiming those for himself if Rose becomes incapacitated. Jim is a strong, self-made man, owner of a very successful plumbing supply company, and the Murphy cousins have never been comfortable with him. He dotes on Lisa, his daughter by his first wife, and as we have seen, the cousins have largely excluded Lisa. If he becomes a partner, it is likely that he will push for her inclusion in any formal agreement about ownership and use of Pine Haven.

Rose and Jim's son-in-law, Gary Schmidt, is very successful in real estate, and he has proposed building a second house on the property to ease the pressure on use of the first house. He would finance it entirely by himself, and asks only that he and Amy have first choice of two weeks on that place, with the rest of its use to be determined by the whole family. This proposal is both attractive and a bit scary to most of the rest of the clan. It would be very nice to have more room, but it seems that it would also establish a precedent of one cousin having priority over the others. And expenses would be greater.

Most are willing to look at the idea; however, George Jr.'s daughter Marlene Murphy is adamantly opposed to it. She is an environmental scientist already concerned about what is happening with increased development of their area of the Allegheny Mountains. The only logical site on the property for another house would be uncomfortably close to the trout stream. She is sure that a septic tank would leach into the stream, which has already had its pristine quality tainted by dwellings upstream. The other cousins recognize her concern but there has been a good deal of resentment toward Marlene in the past. For one thing, her environmentalism is voiced in a particularly strident and critical manner. Worse is the fact that a few years ago, she summarily replaced all electric light bulbs with long-lasting ones, which use less electricity but produce a dimmer light, and threw out the old, mouldy porch furniture. It was falling apart, true, but it was original to Pine Haven and had great sentimental value. To put it nicely, sentiment is not one of Marlene's strong values.

There is one other factor that is a potential problem. For a number of years, cousins Steven and Jason Murphy have used Pine Haven for a week in November for deer hunting. The place is not winterized but they use the fireplace and bring along kerosene heaters. Since they are usually accompanied by some buddies and a fair amount of whiskey has been used to "ward off the cold," there is some concern about the heaters. Of greater concern is the fact that this week has never been taken into account as they negotiate for summer use. This was discussed when the cousins put together their proposal to their parents, but since it immediately produced tension, it was set aside in the interest of achieving some consensus.

NOTES: We won't run you through a set of questions this time: you can do that yourself. What sounds familiar here?

CHAPTER 2
HOW AND WHY SUMMER HOUSES ARE SO IMPORTANT

Regardless of your association with a summer or other vacation house, be you a founder or one of a later generation, you have a strong feeling for your place and a good idea of why your feeling is so strong. You've experienced a lot there, you've sweated and hassled over it, worked with — and perhaps against — parents, siblings, cousins, offspring and assorted other relatives to develop and maintain your rights to enjoy it. You have had a lot of fun there, perhaps as a child as well as an adult. You certainly don't need to be told why summer houses are important. Yet since the reasons for the intense feeling for summer houses are so numerous, and since those reasons have impact on the issues we've discussed, consider what's involved in the following statements from summer house owners. Then write down two or three of your favorite memories, comparable to these:

> I can't remember ever not going there. I thought about it all year long. I remember one summer asking my father how long it would be before we went up there. He said, three weeks. "Three weeks?!" Omigosh, that was just forever! I just couldn't understand how I could wait that long.
>
> When my father was dying, he went to spend that last summer at the place he'd built. We all came through during that time to see him. It was so important that it was there that we saw him. I mean, *it* is "the family home" as his retirement condo is not. I was there when he really started going downhill, and I spent a lot of my vacation that year helping to take care of him, and just spending time with him. I didn't do it so much for recreation but it's a summer I'll always treasure. I was able to give back some of what he'd given to me.
>
> When we got there, grandma had always baked her special peanut butter and raisin cookies. The aroma of those cookies just filled that little cottage. I think I remember that aroma better than anything else from my childhood there.
>
> At 23, I thought I was quite the hotshot. I decided to take our sailboat out in

some pretty cold and heavy winds. I knew that Dad didn't approve – he frowned but didn't say anything. Sure enough, we capsized and fortunately, there was a guy in a motor yacht nearby. He towed us in and as we got close to shore, I saw Dad waiting with a couple of buckets to bail us out. I was kind of dreading what he'd say but he had this funny smile on his face. In one bucket were some glasses and in the other, a bottle of brandy. That brandy sure went down smooth.

We had both been working very hard because we were very worried about our jobs. I think we'd been avoiding each other a lot at home, but when we went to our summer place, it was just the two of us, and no place to escape to. For the first week, it was pretty rough. We were nasty to each other, lots of zingers. One night it all came to head. I said one thing too many and she picked up the dishes she'd just washed and slammed them on the floor. Maybe the blowup that followed was good for us. We yelled and called each other every name in the book. When we finally got too tired to yell anymore, we started to talk. And cry. I think we talked and cried until about four in the morning. Then we went to bed. I don't think I'll ever forget that night. Our daughter was conceived during that next week.

Mom and Dad had this rule when we went to our summer place. We weren't allowed to talk about anything bad that had happened the previous twelve months. It seemed to us kind of artificial but they were very strict about it. I have to admit, we did get along a whole lot better, and I think we all realized how negative we can sometimes get. I'm using the same rule with my kids now.

Our family is now so large (I'm fifth generation), that I get just one week every other year. Certainly I'd like to have more, but that one week is sooooo special! And it's funny – it's not like we do a whole lot – mostly just hang out and be together. But that's enough.

One of our traditions is that we overlap for a couple of days with a sibling at the beginning and end of our stay. It's a good idea for a couple of reasons. One is that you don't have to worry so much about making sure the place is clean and the refrigerator stocked for the next occupants. The more important one is that we stay in touch with each other to a degree that would be impossible any other way. I'm not only much closer to my siblings, but I have a real sense of who my nieces and nephews are.

Our place is small and not much to look at, but it's ours. A few years ago, it was damaged in a big storm. When we looked closely at it, we realized it needed a whole lot of normal maintenance in addition to repairing the damage, paint job, roof, plumbing, etc. Well, all of us are either in construction professionally or do a lot of it on our own, so we decided to all vacation together and really do the place up right. We had to bring tents, sleeping bags, Coleman stoves, and all that. Kids were allowed to play but grown-ups had to work. It was an unholy mess! No one was boss, but everyone thought that they knew it better, or they could do it better than anyone else. Lord, did we fight! But you know, we got it done, and done right, even if we did have to use a committee approach. I don't know how, but we did it. And we're all really proud of it, and proud of each other.

I took it upon myself to make new bedspreads for the ones that had been nibbled by mice. I didn't think there'd be a problem, but my mother-in-law had made the originals. I guess they had sentimental value. For at least eighteen years, family members made subtle, and not-so-subtle remarks about them. If I had known what it would be like, I never would have done it. But two years ago, our son was in a car accident and in a coma for three weeks. Suddenly, all that was forgotten, and they were all there for us. I don't think I could have handled it without their support. Gerry will never be quite the same again, but he's about ninety percent. And I haven't heard a remark about the bedspreads since the accident.

At home, when we were little, my sister and I had an eight o'clock bedtime. At our vacation home, there was only one clock and it was in the kitchen. Sara and I would meander out and casually keep track of the time. But our Mom and Dad seemed to lose track of it. We got to stay up till 8:30 or 9:00, and it was so exciting! We thought we were getting away with something, but now I know that they were always aware of the time. They actually enjoyed our feeling that we'd put one over on them.

It was while we were on vacation that my ex-husband, Ray, and I decided to call it quits. We had gone through counseling but realized that we'd just grown apart. It wasn't an angry divorce, but it was awfully painful. Three years later, Tim and I honeymooned there. My two kids were with us, as was his daughter. I think the fun we all had helped us begin to blend. Blending families is really a bitch, but spending time there has helped a lot.

As kids, we had a rule that we had to do one thing each day to make our place better. It could be pulling up weds, or washing the kitchen floor or for a little one, filling the bird feeder. We hated that rule! Groused, whined and moaned about it, but we could never get out of it. Now when we go there, we have what we call a "Boast Book." Each of us writes in it the repairs and improvements we made during our stay. There's almost a little competition to do more than the other guy, but it does keep the place well maintained.

We have a weekly fee that we all have to pay toward taxes and maintenance. When I lost my job, I knew I couldn't afford the week I was entitled to so I was ready to give it up. My cousins insisted that I take my week and said that they'd pick up the fee. I'm kind of close to a couple of them, but not all - we're scattered all over the east. But they know how important the place is to all of us. I'm really grateful to them.

Sometimes we would get up at dawn and quietly slip outside to observe nature. My folks were bird watchers and animal lovers and they would point things out to us. As sleepy as we were, it was fascinating at that hour, so still, almost eerie. It was amazing how much wildlife you could see in a short time. For various reasons, I now live in the city, but I'm much more sensitive to nature than anyone else I know.

We still went there even when though Kathy was seven and a half months along with our first. It was a short trip and being pregnant during a hot summer was no fun for her. Two days before we were due to go home, she started into labor. I was kicking myself for taking her there, especially seeing the size of the little country hospital we had to go to. Fortunately, everything went smoothly and our son was born without a problem. Now Cory kind of lords it over his cousins and younger siblings. He seems to have more of a proprietary attitude about the place and likes to boast that he's a "native."

When I was sixteen, I used to hitch into town, which was about five miles away. It was easy to get a ride. My folks let me go as long as I was home by ten or called them if I couldn't get a ride. Then they'd come and get me but most of the time, I got a ride. There were a bunch of kids who used to hang out there. Town isn't much, but we'd get ice cream or play pinball or just walk down along the beach. It was just cool to be with other kids without your parents hovering over you.

It was while we were on vacation that I decided to go back to school. It was an easy decision then, when we were relaxed and having fun. I had been fed up with my job and with my boss for a long time, and I just couldn't face going back there. Starting classes at the community college was scary because academics have never been my strong suit. But my wife was real supportive and I found that the years since high school had given me a lot more maturity and motivation. It took four years to finish my associate's degree but I made it. And I'm making more money in a much better job. Each year we go back, we remember sitting by the fire and making that decision.

We used to like to go skinny dipping. It was always easy during the day to decide that we'd do it that evening, and then the cool air of evening would arrive and we'd start to regret the decision. But someone would always egg the others on, calling them "chicken" and making clucking noises. So we'd have a fire going in the fireplace and wrap towels around us. We'd run down to the lake and throw ourselves in, squealing and yapping about the cold. We'd get fully wet, splash around, then dash back to the house and sit before the fire. Mom would get out the chocolate and marshmallow makings for "s'mores" and we'd do them at the fire. It made the cold water worth it. One night my smartass brother Sean brought a flash camera down to the lake. He took three or four pictures as we dashed in and when we realized what he was doing, we dashed out and chased him. We didn't realize he hadn't stripped and he had his sneakers on, so we couldn't catch him. Besides, it was hard running while holding a towel around you. We waited up for him to come back but he snuck in during the wee hours of the morning. The next day, dad opened the camera and took out the film, over Sean's loud protests. For the rest of the vacation, Sean was a marked man.

YOUR MEMORIES: Some have probably occurred to you as you read these. Mull them over for a moment, then write down one from your youth, and one that is more recent.

The obvious theme in all these remarks is "family." Summer houses are "family" houses, sometimes more than the year-round home. As one woman told Judy, "It's where we *do* family." These are the places of our strongest memories, childhood and adult; they're where we grew up, where we encountered and resolved problems, where we reconfigured family constellations, and where we had family gatherings that had become more difficult as families spread across the range of the country and of interests and thus impossible to hold anywhere else that didn't have the collective memories we all have in our specific summer house.

They are also where we have always had the most fun. As children, this fun was quite literally "care-free." Maybe this is one reason why we may have difficulty managing the place as adults. Now we know just how much care it really takes and resent the fact.

Of course, it's not just the house that needs care; it's actually easier than the family. We can hire people to fix the problems that time and nature cause. With family, though, we create and inherit the problems, and there's no one whom we can hire who can fix these problems alone, not even our friendly neighborhood family therapist. He or she may help us find ways to resolve the difficulties, but we have to do the hard work ourselves. A summer house owner of our acquaintance has helped a few families work out agreements. He said, half facetiously, that if he were to go into this professionally, he would start a consulting firm, including "one lawyer, half an accountant, and five family therapists," to go out and make site visits.

We don't know that it would take five therapists. If they were working for the same firm, they might develop some interesting dynamics themselves. Yet we wouldn't need an Alfred Adler, the father of family therapy, or one of his disciples, to recognize the tremendous complexity of an extended family, and it's potential for serious interpersonal problems. Knots and thorns are not just found in vegetation; they grow in families, too.

It is because our summer house is so important that conflicts and difficulties that might lie under the surface are brought to the light and exacerbated. If while growing up, my brother and I were often antagonistic, we would probably learn to peacefully coexist as we became more mature and saw each other seldom. We could keep our conflict under control over Thanksgiving Dinner, or during my daughter's wedding reception. Yet if we both want to spend Labor Day weekend at our summer place, and there isn't room for the both of us, that old antagonism may prove to be very much alive.

If you are one of the third, fourth or fifth generation with some claim on a summer house, you may be all too aware of this. If you are a founder or second generation, you might take offense at some of what we've said: *your* children and grandchildren are certainly not going to have such problems! Well, we certainly hope so. Yet you can't be sure of this. You don't know how times will change, what problems your children and theirs will encounter, who they will marry, what their in-laws and their children will be like, etc.

In our experience, few founders think much beyond what their grandchildren might do with the summer house. This is certainly understandable, but it is also unfortunate; after all, none of them plans to have the house sold off as soon as they die and they try to make provision for its interim future, hopefully before their great-grandchildren (who are second cousins) are old enough to have a claim to the place. Summer houses are much too precious to have their fate left to chance. They become the focus of all that is good — and much that is bad in our families. As succeeding generations take their place, in turn taking *our* place, they inherit some of the good we leave them, and a lot of the bad, ditto. They shouldn't be expected to resolve things all by themselves when they are cousins, or second cousins, or cousins once removed, or step-cousins, or whatever. They need a formal plan, one that everyone has bought into, that can guide them through the storms and shoals, the straits and narrows of owning, maintaining and using their special summer place.

CHAPTER 3
TYPES OF OWNERSHIP AND INFORMAL USE AGREEMENTS AND WHAT MAKES THEM WORK

Here we briefly review the various legal forms of joint ownership and operation of an entity such as a summer house. Our discussion is in no way exhaustive of the various forms, nor of the nuances of any single one. It is just to introduce you to your options, not to spell them out in detail.

The Madison and Murphy families are representatives of two types of informal family ownership of summer houses. For reasons which may already be evident, but which we, being pedants, will explain nevertheless, neither of these is adequate for peaceful ownership and use of a summer house through multiple generations.

SINGLE OR JOINT OWNERSHIP

The Madisons represent this type, which almost all families begin with and some maintain long past its usefulness. One or two individuals own the property. Founders are almost always joint owners, and in some cases, as the property passes to the second generation, one or two siblings inherit as the only beneficiaries of inheritance. In other instances, one or two siblings may have been able to buy out the others.

Decision-making and handling financial obligations may be fairly easy to do with only one or two individuals holding power. However, this style only defers problems to the next generation. Since they are likely to be larger in number, it is less likely that one or two can buy the others out to reduce the pool of decision-makers. Moreover, since they have grown up going to the summer houses and having all decisions made for them, they may be ill-prepared psychologically for the mantle of ownership. There are instances of individuals not being given any responsibility for ownership until they were in their forties or fifties. While they may be worldly-wise in other ways, they may still be under-prepared to handle the complexities of family ownership.

These complexities are multiplied by the fact that members of the third generation are likely to be more distant from each other, both experientially and geographically, than were their sibling parents. Some first cousins may be close, while others little more than strangers with familiar names. Even for those who are close, there may not be the commitment to each other that derives from having grown up and vacationed together.

It is true that average family size is shrinking so that there may be just as many second generation members as third, yet this phenomenon of demographics is partially offset by a second trend when it comes to who has claim to a family's identity: divorce, remarriage and blending families have become more common, and as we saw with the Murphys, these events add other spices to the family stew.

At some point, maybe with the second generation and almost inevitably by the third, Single or Joint Ownership becomes impossible. Unfortunately, this point too often comes with painful ramifications. If family members cannot buy each other out or agree on a formal pattern of ownership, the family summer house may be sold, each member receiving a modest or even healthy chunk of change, but one inadequate for healing the emotional wounds that he or she may have received from the very process that results in the sale. Even if one or two cousins are able to buy out the others, the latter may be resentful, even bitter, that through choices of vocation and lifestyle they have lost their part of a special place of their youth. The one or two now in possession have also not resolved the problems: they have merely ensured that they will be visited on their children and grandchildren.

INFORMAL "COMPLEX" OWNERSHIP

The Murphys exemplify this common style of ownership, usually involving second and third generation, though we have found it extending into the fourth generation. With this type of ownership, a trust provides for the expenses so that there has been no need for the heirs to take over the financial obligations of maintaining the property. They are free to perpetuate a semi-formal structure for handling use and physical management of the place. Members are in agreement on these practices, based on "how Mom and Dad did it" or "wanted it." Tradition is the keynote here, and it is a powerful and often useful basis for decisions.

However, as these generations pass on to that Great Summer House in the Sky, much of their authority and the power of tradition goes with them. Third and certainly fourth generation members may have never known the founders or had any feeling for them. To them, the founders may be nothing more than hoary ancestors whose mythical words have lost their original meaning and become just a burden. How great-grandpa and great-grandma did it, or wanted it done, may be of little use sixty or eighty years later to a much enlarged generation of first- and second-cousins. Even if the mythical words of the founders are kept alive by strong family ties and traditions, they are not likely to help an extended family of twenty or twenty-five members divide up a summer, or divide up the cost or responsibility of maintaining the place.

If Informal Complex Ownership goes into the fourth generation (and our evidence suggests that this can happen only due to luck), those members may realize that it is no longer working. Yet it may be difficult for them all to get together and agree on a method of Formal Ownership. We are not alone in believing that this should be done earlier, and if you are a second or third generation member, you probably realize this. At the same time, informal agreements are to be prized, not denigrated: they are the basis of the formal agreements that should emerge. Why?

THE IMPORTANCE OF INFORMAL USE AGREEMENTS

While we recommend *some* type of formal agreement for ownership, maintenance and use of a summer house (see below), it is essential that there also be a successfully working informal system of use and maintenance. In practice, the informal always precedes the formal and families do not simply junk what they had to start from a *tabula rasa*. They take what has worked, adding procedures and issues such as rental that have not been previously and informally agreed upon. As your family probably has a summer house (why else would you be reading this?) you could probably write much of what follows. You may in fact be able to identify some important characteristics that make a system work or fail, so we'll leave some space for you to jot these down.

In her discussions with over 125 respondent-owners of summer houses, Judy has found certain features of *successful* informal ownership and use agreements that are fairly consistent. Among these are that:

The implicit authority of the system is recognized and honored by all family members. If the family has always met during the Christmas season to decide summer slots, one member doesn't make travel plans to the summer house prior to the meeting.

Founders and other senior family members begin delegating responsibility to the next generation as they achieve maturity, not when the seniors die or become incapable of handling it.

Children grow up contributing to the well-being of the house and maintain the habit of working on and for it, not just enjoying it.

Some kind of "log" is kept of each member's contributions of maintenance and repair. This demonstrates commitment and can lead to a positive and implicit sense of competition, e.g. "So Cousin Fred cleaned all the windows inside and out? Well, I'm going to clean and straighten out the shed and garage — which is an even dirtier job, so I'll get 'bragging points' at the Christmas family meeting."

There is a check-off list of tasks to be done to make the place ready for the next users, as well as of seasonally-determined tasks related to opening and closing.

Family members communicate throughout the year, and not just about the house. They have a sense of who each other is and what their lives are like.

Overlapping slots among family members are frequent. While not necessary, there are many advantages to them. Members can discuss things that need to be done and work on them together . They can learn different ways to enjoy their property. And they can develop a better sense of what each other is like than is possible over the traditional Thanksgiving dinner.

OTHER TYPES OF SUCCESSFUL INFORMAL PRACTICES THAT YOU ARE PRESENTLY DOING:

If your informal agreement seems to be less than satisfactory and even if you can identify some of the reasons why, it's not easy to simply sit down and rewrite it. These patterns have grown up over years and generations, and represent the attitudes and values of many people. However, recognizing that a successful informal agreement is a necessary precursor to a successful formal one, there are certain steps you could take to improve the family climate.

One simple way would be to communicate more with family members during the rest of the year. Learn more of what they're doing, share what your nuclear family is doing, and do not get into issues over the summer house. There will be time for that later.

If you haven't had one before, you could also begin a "work log" next summer, including not only what you have done, but noting what those who preceded you did. And if your children have not been required to put in some sweat equity on a regular basis, you might start them doing this next summer. It won't be easy; they'll certainly squawk, but stick to your guns. It might help if they knew that some of their cousins were being required to work during their own slot.

CHAPTER 4
TYPES OF FORMAL OWNERSHIP AND USE AGREEMENTS: WHY THEY ARE NECESSARY

In this chapter, we want to discuss the pros and cons of various formal, legal agreements, and make some recommendations. Before doing so, we would like to recommend that you also take a look at *Preserving Family Lands I and II (1992; 1997)*, both by attorney Stephen J. Small and published by the Landowner Planning Center in Boston. He describes different ways through which you can donate aspects of the use of your land to a non-profit organization while retaining its use for you and your family, such as a conservation easement. By doing so, you not only get an immediate tax deduction for a charitable donation, but you also protect against ruinous inheritance taxes by reducing the assessable value of the property. Inheritance is probably the single biggest unacknowledged issue that families face; at least, it is the one that will most quickly eliminate the possibility of owning and using a summer house. Small's books are short and easily read and understood; we think they are both a useful adjunct to what we are discussing.

However, none of Small's suggestions deal with the other kinds of issues we are discussing, and following any one of the alternatives for a legal structure will not be sufficient in itself for your family to use and maintain your summer house to your greatest benefit. You will need another agreement that, for example, determines how it will be decided who gets the July 4th weekend.

State laws regarding trusts, partnerships, associations and corporations vary, so you will need to do some research on how they operate in the state where your summer house is located as well as in your own, in terms of inheritance taxes. You should certainly consult an attorney, and we recommend that you talk with one in the region of your summer house. While he or she may not wear the wing-tipped oxfords of a big city attorney, he or she is likely to be more aware of ownership patterns in your summer neighborhood. This is particularly true if there are a number of summer houses where yours is located. It's possible that this small town attorney has much of his or her practice with summer house owners. Talking to other owners who have local attorneys is, of course, a good idea.

We cannot urge you strongly enough to work out most of the details of your intended agreement *before* consulting the attorney. You don't need to pay an attorney's hourly fee to help you and your family decide how to allocate summer slots. Besides, it won't be feasible for the entire family to sit down with that attorney. Work out the details among yourselves; be sure that everyone has agreed to the procedures to be formalized. We know of instances where a couple of good-hearted souls took it upon themselves to formalize what they "thought" the family consensus was. The resulting legal document was submitted to the rest of the family, only to be immediately eviscerated. And, as any surgeon can tell you, evisceration is a bloody procedure.

In Chapter 6, we will discuss how to go about drafting a formal agreement, but now, let's look at the different types of formal ownership systems. (A more detailed discussion of these systems may be found in Chapter 13 of Judy's book, *Passing It On: The Inheritance and Use of Summer Houses.* Stephen J. Small gives a particularly good summary in his second book, but again focusing on legal and tax issues rather than the family issues which we are considering here.)

TRUSTS

There are various types of trusts, and they are most often established by the founders of a summer house. They typically provide an endowment to cover anticipated taxes and maintenance costs. Procedures for using the house may be set down but often these are vague, or do *not* anticipate the size of the third and fourth generations, let alone the inevitably increased size of "third or fourth generation" taxes.

Though the founders may feel good about establishing a trust, there are a number of problems with this structure. As just noted, if real estate values increase rapidly, as they often do in resort areas, the money in the endowment may be inadequate to pay for taxes, or even maintenance. Second, the terms of any trust are rigid; they can't be easily amended as conditions may warrant. Third generation members may chafe and conflict under procedures that were fine for the second generation. For example, the terms of a trust are unlikely to spell out how twelve families should divide up the private summer slots nor even provide for a process for replacing trustees, with equable representation among extended family lines or generations.

Third, the trust expires when the last person named in it dies. This may be in the fourth generation, when a number of second cousins, many of whom don't know each other well, find they have no agreement among themselves for maintaining their summer house. Fourth, a trust does not protect descendants from inheritance taxes, which, we rather painfully found ourselves, can be extremely large on second homes. Finally, founders usually establish the terms by themselves. Those who must live by them have had no say in their determination. As we will discuss later, agreements which all parties have "bought into" by being involved in their development are the most likely to work successfully.

If you are a founder who is considering a trust, we recommend that you talk to your children and grandchildren, if they are old enough, and then to an attorney about adding an additional type of agreement, like an association. If you are a second or third generation member who abides under a trust and sees problems with it, we recommend that you talk with your siblings and/or cousins about a supplemental agreement that will continue when the trust ends. Then go talk to your friendly neighborhood lawyer.

PARTNERSHIPS

Partnerships look attractive to many families because they are fairly easy to set up. They are commonly established with second and sometimes third generation members. Typically, each direct heir in the second generation constitutes one "share" of the partnership, and as such, there is an apparent fairness and equality among the several "lines" of the family. One share, one vote, and everyone have equal say. Strangely enough, the apparent fairness can mask an inherit inequity. This can develop with a partnership because of the one person-one share idea, and because of our American egalitarian pattern of offspring inheriting equal portions of estates. For example, if I have three children but my sister has just one, when I die each of my children will have one-third of the share, while their cousins will have a whole one. (This only happens if inheritance of shares by heirs is stipulated. Under some partnership agreements, surviving partners inherit a deceased partner's share; in other words, my sister rather than my children would inherit my share.) That only child cousin's "piece of the pie" is larger and of greater value than my children's.

This inequity can be obviated to a degree by taking in all of the cousins as new partners at some point, yet if we do that, my family "line" will wield greater clout than my sister's. Moreover, a partnership with twenty or more partners may be rather cumbersome, even if some are senior partners (the siblings) and others junior partners (the cousins). In an association or corporation, all members of a particular generation can be given the same number of shares, and while my line may still have greater clout, the individual cousins will have equal pieces of the pie.

At the same time, one advantage of partnerships is that buy-outs of other individuals may be facilitated, since it's simply one share that is being bought. On the other hand, partial buy-outs would be more difficult or even impossible, and the price of a buy-out of a single share may be more than any single family member can afford.

One problem with a system of partnership shares (which pertains also to the associations and corporations we discuss below) is that it is extremely difficult to establish a permanent "shares-to-use" equation. We are aware of only one family that has done this successfully. Does a share entitle you to one week per summer? Or ten days? Sounds relatively easy, you say? Well, which week? Will it be one of the nine July and August "prime" weeks? What if there are seven partners? Or eleven? How would the equation work then? How will succeeding generations be taken care of by the equation? Even if one can deal with equal numbers of days of use, what of priorities based on different needs of the users (school or summer camp schedules for one's children; work schedules for adults permitting only the last two weeks in August for a vacation — when that is the only time the water is warm enough for other family members to enjoy)?

Such a series of rhetorical question is bad writing, and we apologize, but they illustrate one of the most frustrating issues of any formal agreement, and one that must be discussed at some length. Any solution of this equation must anticipate the increase in family size that will occur as other generations come along.

To get back to partnerships, there are a few other problems with them. One is that because they are easy to set up, they are less likely to address the various issues we have alluded to and which are spelled out in the next chapter. They are more likely to be merely financial agreements, not usage and maintenance ones.

Another problem is that there are unlikely to be any tax benefits, as there may be with associations and corporations. Such benefits will vary from state-to-state and presidential campaign to presidential campaign, and are something to be researched and considered in the process of drafting a formal agreement. For example, as members die and shares are inherited, the heirs will be subject to inheritance taxes on the value of those shares. If the property is worth $500,000 and there are five partners, the heirs of one who dies will have to pay inheritance taxes on $100,000. In an association or corporation with multiple shares, some of these can be gifted to the next generation before death and probate, thus reducing the inheritance tax.

Perhaps most important is the fact that a partnership does not protect its members from liability problems. If I have a guest who falls off the deck, fractures his frabijam, and files a ten million-dollar suit against the partnership (we who collectively own the property) for "terminal humiliation," *all* of us are personally liable. Our own homes, our businesses, even Grandpa's old raccoon coat may be attached to pay for our "negligence." The liability issue is particularly important if the property is ever going to be rented. Renters would be more likely to sue than would be our dear friends whom we have invited to share our place out of the goodness of our warm hearts. Slightly more likely.

ASSOCIATIONS

An association is an unincorporated legal organization with formal by-laws which can spell out all the usage and maintenance procedures. Individual members may own multiple shares, which may vary by generation, second generation individuals owning more than third, and so on. Purchase of a few shares, of part of individuals' holdings, is possible, but here the "shares-to-use" problem can become even stickier. If I sell twenty of my sixty shares to my brother, how much more time should he get than I do?

One of the advantages of an association comes from the fact that it is the association that owns the property. Only the association can be sued for a liability problem. As with a corporation, ditto, any such successful suit can take only the assets — the summer house itself — not the private property of the individual association members or corporate owners. Further, because individuals own multiple shares, it's possible to minimize inheritance tax burdens. As I hit the autumn and then winter of my years, I can gradually gift my shares to my children, as long as they understand that I do not thereby relinquish my usage rights! Deference to senior family members is expected, after all! Depending on the value of the property and of the shares, I can give each child "x" number per year without their having to pay a gift tax, perhaps even giving more to the most deferential.

Many families have established an association and found it to be a very workable system. One major drawback must be noted: as with a trust, the governance of an association is not automatically established as it is with a corporation. Officers do not have to be elected, and association meetings are not required.

These could, however, be put into your by-laws, should you decide on this type of agreement. If a "CEO" is to be designated, we suggest that the position be rotated periodically, perhaps every three years. If your family is larger, with a number of lines and members of lines, you might want to have each line choose a representative, those selected then becoming a governing council. Again, the position of council member could be rotated within a line.

CORPORATIONS

A corporation has all the benefits of an association, plus some additional ones. While it is more complex and more costly to establish in terms of immediate legal fees, we feel that it is the best of the various types of formal legal ownership in many situations. In addition to the benefits described above, there may be added tax benefits to share owners, but there may also be tax deficits (on which account Stephen J. Small advises against use of this structure, ignoring some of the family-centered reasons why it may be the least-worst option.) The tax situation of all potential owners should be taken into account when this option is considered, especially if the summer house is unlikely to be rented and thus generate a business profit (or "break-even") on which basis corporations normally operate.

There are two basic types of corporations. In an "S" corporation, shareholders directly receive any profits or are responsible for losses, and they pay taxes on their profits. In a "C" corporation, it is the corporation itself which gets the profits or suffers the losses, and it pays any related taxes at outset, with any remaining profits or losses, now presumably reduced, passed on to the shareholders as part of their own individual tax base. There is inevitably a corporate bank account (perhaps established by a trust or an estate) which is the where-with-all to pay the bills. Naturally, among the corporate officers to be elected, there would have to be a "Chief Financial Officer."

As fairly elaborate corporate bylaws are likely to be set up at outset, a "buy-sell agreement" can limit the number of shares that can be purchased, thus protecting family members who are not as well off as others. It could also be decided that the corporation would issue new shares as new members of the family are born, thereby reducing the value of each share. On the other hand, it could be decided to limit the total number of shares, meaning that new members would have to wait to inherit the shares of their parents. In any event, such corporate shares might be subject to less of an inheritance tax burden since the corporation may preset their value. Each share may be valued at something less than the percentage of the current property value which it represents.

Corporate governance may be facilitated more easily than in other legal structures because a corporation *must* elect officers and hold an annual meeting, to which all shareholders must be invited. Offices again may be rotated among family members. While such an operation may seem successively formal and cold to some, particularly to a Ginger Madison who wants everyone to "listen with love in their hearts," which corporations are not noted for doing, it increases the chances that a family will operate in a caring but dispassionate manner. Nothing prevents shareholders from listening with love; being part of a corporation does not necessarily lead one to become robber baron.

We feel that especially for a large family, getting into the third, fourth and fifth generation with adult interest in the summer house, a corporation may well be the best system despite — or perhaps because of — its legal complexity. And remember that even if you are of the second or third generation, you undoubtedly hope that your children, and their children will love and enjoy your summer house as much as you have. Establishing a corporation will help ensure that, if the other implications of its tax structure make sense to you.

There are other legal forms, or versions of the above categories, which may be appropriate for you in your situation. Our major point is that you should review the options and discuss them among yourselves before you go to your lawyer of choice. A second point is that you keep the legal structure as simple, and as remediable, as possible. Working agreements about implementation can be changed as situations warrant without having to involve lawyers and the courts. Your job is to provide a firm structure but let your heirs deal with the details in a flexible manner, as seems best to them under circumstances you cannot even imagine. (What??? Sell off the back twenty acres in order to sustain the lakeside ten???! Impossible!! — but for your heirs, maybe necessary.)

CHAPTER 5

ISSUES TO BE ADDRESSED IN AN OPERATING AGREEMENT

In this chapter, we will identify the issues that you will likely have to address in a formal operating agreement. You have probably been grappling with them in your existing informal agreement, but in a formal agreement, the policies that pertain to them need to be more specific. Even if you have existing policies which have worked well, we feel that it is better that you be explicit rather than assume that a strong existing consensus precludes the need for this. Remember that such a consensus may not exist in succeeding generations, and even among your own if you but ask.

To start with, the formal operating agreement should state explicitly what everyone else says they already accept. Here again, you may be very much aware of many or most of these issues. Many of them are implicit or explicit in the Madison and Murphy stories, or in the comments from summer house users Judy has talked with. Nevertheless, we are listing them to serve as a checklist for you to use as you go through the process of drafting such an agreement. We have written them in the form of questions, with some explanatory space where necessary. We are also leaving space after each issue for you to note the particular ideas, questions, and contingencies that may be pertinent to your situation. You might want to include what your current practice is.

There are certainly issues that we haven't encountered or thought of but which you know all too well, so we are leaving space at the end of this chapter for you to note them. If you do, try to put them in general terms of objective behavior, of what can be clearly seen, heard and attested to. In other words, avoid saying, "That spoiled brat cousin of mine just has to have her !@#$%^&* way every time we decide on slots." Even saying, "Stacy has had first choice in slots two of the last three years, and some of her cousins have expressed anger about this," is not as objective, nor as helpful, as wording it, "Some cousins appear to others to have been prioritized in their choice of slots, and the other cousins are unhappy about this." (Granted: the language here makes it sound as if a bureaucrat wrote it, but there are advantages to the neutrality of bureaucratic language: things happen but no individual is responsible for that happening, so no one individual can be blamed. You know why that is sometimes useful, and sometimes not.)

Whatever the language of expression, there are three general areas to be addressed in any formal operating agreement: time-sharing, work and cost sharing, and governance. As we run through the related specific questions here, you should note your current practice and why it does, or doesn't, seem to work. Further, if it works now, how will it work in a dozen years or so when the next generation is older?

ISSUES TO BE ADDRESSED IN A WORKING AGREEMENT:

How many "slots" per summer will there be and how long is each slot?

Will slots overlap, or run contiguously, i.e. Sunday morning to Saturday night?

How is the allocation of slots decided, and by whom?

Whether or not there may be more "family units" than slots, how are slots to be assigned or rotated? (A family unit may be anything from a single person and friends, the traditional nuclear family, or a senior heir with children and grandchildren expected to share the place together.)

Are certain slots more valuable than others? For example, July 4th and Labor Day weekends are very popular. If you get one, do you have to give something up the next time?

What about early and late season slots? If one family unit can take one and no one else can (perhaps because they don't have school-age children), can they also be eligible for a prime slot? Are late season slots more advantageous (warmer water, fewer flies) than early, and how should this be compensated?

If I can't or choose not to take my slot when eligible, do I get first choice next year or do I "lose my place in line?"

Who opens and closes the house at the beginning and end of the season? How is this paid for if someone is hired? If family members perform the task, will their compensation be a longer slot, or one in more prime time?

As the next generation comes along, at what point, e.g. marriage, death of parents, do they get to have their own slot as opposed to sharing with their parents'?

If the founders are still alive, what can be done now to forestall ruinous inheritance taxes that might force the sale of the house? This will vary from state to state but the question is at the heart of our recommendation, discussed in the previous chapter, to develop a formal agreement leading to an association or corporation.

How is the "shares-to-use" equation going to be formulated and operate?

Will there be a "users' fee" per slot to cover the taxes and maintenance? If not, how will each family be assessed their share? Who will serve as financial manager? Should this position be rotated?

What happens if one family unit, due to loss of job, severe illness, etc., is unable to pay their yearly share?

If one family unit wants to be bought out, can this be required of the other members?

If there is to be a buy-out, will the rest of the family do this, or just one or two members? (We recommend that this be a "total family" undertaking whenever possible, whatever the formal legal structure of essentially "calling in the shares."

If this is to be an association or corporation with multiple shares, is a partial buy-out possible? How many shares could be bought? What would this mean in terms of use?

Will a sell-out to non-family be prohibited? We recommend that this be the case. Few if any families permit it. You wouldn't want anyone who would be interested in buying in, other than an in-law — and maybe not even then!

Who oversees maintenance and takes the responsibility of seeing that major repairs are completed?

How will an expensive repair, such as a new roof, be paid for?

Is it possible to remodel, expand, and add to the house? At what point might this be desirable? How are the When, Where, How, Who Pays, questions to be decided? Without question, this is a family decision and family undertaking, though it is likely that one member will have more need and/or means to do it. If one member does it, it will give him/her implicit precedence in all decisions regarding the place, and everyone will know this. It may be difficult for the family to do it, and more difficult for them to decide how it should be done, but it will be better in the long run.

What plans could/should be made to make the house more accessible for a family member who is disabled, either through accident or disease, or through the debility of old age? This is particularly important given the small size of many houses, and the problem is more common than you might think.

What happens if a major appliance gives up the ghost during one slot and must be replaced immediately? (As you probably know, this happens all too often, It's tough on appliances to stand idle for nine months and then receive heavy use for three.) Who decides on which new refrigerator or range and how it will be paid for?

How and by whom is it to be decided when furnishings and furniture must be replaced and with what? (This can be among the stickiest of question. People develop strong attachments to their favorite chair, couch, etc.) If Silvia Madison decides to make some new teal/magenta/canary/salmon drapes, does the family have to use them?

Who handles legal matters such as any changes in deeds, assessments, and taxes, particularly during the off season?

How should those handling the responsibilities mentioned above be compensated with slot time, if at all?

Should these positions be rotated? If so, how?

What is "sweat equity" worth and when does it go beyond normal duties? If my wife and I clean out the old barn during our slot, what is our compensation beyond a feeling of satisfaction? It is unlikely that any formula can be devised for normal duties. It might be decided to compensate major jobs, such as house painting or re-roofing.

Will a log be kept of normal tasks and jobs each family unit has done?

May certain slots be rented by the whole family to outsiders so as to provide funds for taxes and maintenance? How will this happen? Who will serve as landlord?

Can individual family units rent their slot? To whom? Who gets the rental fee? Can individual family units let non-family members use their slot or part of it as a gift? (This is sometimes done as a wedding present or donation to a charity auction.)

If elderly family members can no longer use their slots alone, with whom will they stay when they come? How will those members be compensated?

Will any property, e.g. a sailboat, be reserved for one family and off limits for others?

What rules will there be regarding pets? For instance, some families require that members who bring dogs also "flea bomb" the house as they depart. What if certain members have animal allergies and follow those with furry pets? What of the use of pesticides or other means of destroying vermin, to which some have ethical or other objections?

Will sensible environmental practices be required, such as recycling? What about more extreme measures, such as the use of only biodegradable cleaning products and long-life (but dim) light bulbs? What about more expensive measures, such as replacing an imperfectly functioning septic system? These are important questions. Many summer houses are located in environments that can be easily damaged by even minor amounts of pollutants, but summer house residents may be unaware of this. In this regard, when should use of the composting toilet or the privy be required? Any special dispensations on grounds of sex, age, or terror of spiders?

What will be the formal status of in-laws, stepbrothers and sisters? In the event of the death of one of the "blood" relatives, can the surviving widow or widower assume his/her role, or will it pass to the offspring? If to the offspring, how old would they have to be?

At what point will members of the older generation "retire" and hand over their responsibilities to the next generation?

How can the by-laws dealing with these and any other issues be amended when conditions warrant?

ANY OTHER ISSUES WE HAVEN'T MENTIONED???

CHAPTER 6
HOW TO GO ABOUT DEVELOPING A FORMAL AGREEMENT

Okay, we've convinced you of the necessity of making a formal agreement and you're champing at the bit to get going. How should you go about this? Of course, there's no magic sequence since families differ so much, but we can offer some guidelines.

First, recognize that it's going to take a lot longer than you would hope. Doing it within a year would be extremely optimistic. It will probably get frustrating and it may get infuriating, but remember that the time and hard work put in now will pay off. It will produce an agreement that all family members will be able to live with because they have all had their say.

Second, work to include all family members of any degree of maturity. If you are a founder, don't impose a system from the top down. Talk with your offspring and descendants, even if they are still adolescents. They may not have much idea of what would be the best rental policy, for instance, but the process of deriving an agreement is highly educational, and someday, they will be in charge. Their education can't begin too early.

Though the agreement should not be imposed, drafting one will require two or three people willing to push it, to call other family members and listen to their ideas, to record and digest them, to remind members to respond in writing to a draft of an agreement, identify when there is a consensus, and so on. It would be good if these "pushers" were of different generations so that more members will feel directly represented. While it may not be possible to have different generations, different ages and life situations may make the process seem more representative.

If you decide to have a family meeting, those calling it should not preside. The "callers" may have the most vested interest in the house and may not be seen as neutral. The "presider" should be someone seen by all as neutral, perhaps even a trusted in-law. Recognize that in-laws are, at very least, "silent partners" to the heirs in the direct line, and while they may be silent among other members of the extended family, they are not silent with their spouse, the heir. Their views should be solicited and included in the discussion, even if they have no formal, voting rights.

Speaking of generations, if there is a generation older than yours, you might start with trying to get your elders interested in developing an agreement, and then letting them talk to their offspring, your siblings and cousins. At the same time, don't let them carry the ball for you: show that you are respecting the elders but not relying upon them to do the organizing work.

Keep gender bias out of the process. Men may not take more naturally to any such discussion than do women, but they may try to dominate it out of rivalry with each other. Make a point to include sisters, daughters or nieces, not their husbands, even if one of the latter may be a partner in a Wall Street law firm or CEO of a Fortune 500 corporation — and vice versa, if she is the partner and he is the "child care-giver." Actually, especially if he or she is such a partner or CEO. All family members are to be seen as equal in this discussion regardless of age (assuming they have reached legal and social maturity), sex, or occupation. This raises the issue of deciding to exclude any who are not legally or socially responsible for themselves, and why. You have to resolve that one on the basis of individual abilities, not abstract principles, and it won't be easy if you have any such disabled family members.

Generally, while an in-law may preside, in-laws have little or no official say in developing an agreement, unless they are a surviving spouse speaking for children who are direct descendants.

Recognize that some members may be antagonistic to the whole process. Like Ginger Madison, they may feel that it is somehow anti-romantic, akin to writing a pre-nuptial agreement. If Cousin Grace says that she doesn't want to be involved, don't preclude her later involvement. Don't get angry but do tell her that you would welcome her input at any point in the process. On the other hand, if Cousin Leo says that it's fine to do this but he really doesn't care what goes into the agreement, try to encourage his involvement by asking about points you think are really important to him. If you know that he loves the shingled exterior of the house, ask how he'd feel if two or three other members wanted to install vinyl siding.

As we discussed in Chapter 3, you know that during this process, old tensions, wounds, conflicts, etc. are likely to resurface and obstruct progress. If your family and its informal agreement have had problems, this should not preclude you from trying to work on a formal agreement. You and yours will certainly know where the sticky issues are. The process of developing a formal agreement will force you to talk about the problems that have existed, but which people have probably not talked about in other than peevish and angry tones. Hopefully, the discussion can be calm and objective and progress will be made, both toward an agreement and toward a family that works together better.

If you are one of the ones initiating the process, it is essential that you model the kind of behavior that is required, even if you have very painful and legitimate grievances against other family members. Stay calm, bite your tongue, truly listen (ideally with love in your heart), explain over and over if necessary, acknowledge hurts, complaints, differing opinions, and keep your focus on what is best for all the family.

In other words, model yourself after St. Francis of Assisi, Mohandas Gandhi, Eleanor Roosevelt, Martin Luther King, or whatever patron saint of serenity and understanding you wish. The scars on your tongue will be your badges of honor.

As to those other members who insist on being difficult, try to anticipate what the problems will be and work to defuse them without letting the process become one massive group therapy session. Keep the focus on the task, e.g. “Yeah, I know he still treats you like his baby sister, and that's wrong, but that's something you'll have to work out in a different time and place. Right now, we need to decide how slots are going to be allocated.”

Of course, you could also work to improve the underlying *informal* agreement by following the suggestions made in Chapter 3. Focusing on routines that all have accepted in the past will help to restore a task-oriented focus on the present issues to be resolved.

As to getting the formal agreement on paper, you might begin by asking all family members of a certain age to write a "Mission Statement." Corporations, non-profit organizations and educational institutions often have these and they can serve as a guiding philosophy, much as the Preamble to the Constitution does. Such a Statement may, in the words of one of Judy's respondents, professional mediator Louis R. Matlack with offices in Camden, NJ:

> Express an ideal concept of maximum family benefit from shared use of the place, in terms of the collective interest without regard to the sense of comparative power or rights that individuals may have.

Among the questions that such a mission statement might address include:

What is most important to you about our summer house?

What do you value most about your family and how you use it?

How would you like to see the ownership of our house affecting the ways we interact as family members?

A second or simultaneous step might be writing a draft of what you believe that informal agreement is in fact, and then circulating this to see if others concur. Make it absolutely clear that you are describing what you believe the procedures *are*, not necessarily what they should be. Family members whose perceptions are different should be encouraged to write down how they see the family operating.

If this can be done at a family meeting, that would make it easier, but this is not always possible. If it isn't, phone calls work better than letters. Faxes and especially e-mail really speed up this process, so if you don't all own computers, this might be a good reason to take the plunge. E-mail will also facilitate yearly operation of your summer house, and that in itself may be sufficient to motivate some of the family Luddites to prepare for the millennium by getting a computer and on the Internet.

If there are issues, such as rental, for which there have been no implicit or explicit policies, you could then ask for suggestions as to what members think these should be. If they have no idea, offer them options of ways other families have handled the particular issue. Set up a sub-committee to report back. All of this may require a little research on your part. Judy's *Passing It On* would be a good place to start.

For policies that have not worked well and may need changing, suggest some alternatives and ask for responses. In this situation (and in all others) work toward compromise and consensus rather than simple majority rule. This is harder but the payoff is worth it. If there are members who are consistently in the minority on votes, and who feel that their opinions have not "been listened to" (which really means they haven't actually influenced policy), they could later sabotage or refuse to abide by the majority's decisions.

However, if consensus proves impossible, it is better to operate by majority rule than to give individuals the implicit veto power that can develop if complete consensus is required on every point. If we say that all twenty family members must agree — that nineteen are not enough— then we allow one "deviant" to exercise a veto. This can make the whole process extremely tedious, if not impossible. We do know of a couple of families where the unanimity principle operates, but these are families where all members share powerful religious principles supporting such consensus-deriving processes.

As you go through each issue, it might be helpful to distinguish between reluctant acquiescence to the majority as opposed to outright opposition. In other words, there's a difference between saying, "I disagree but I'll go along with it," and

"Over my dead body will you..."

Gradually you are working toward a complete draft of an agreement. If you are doing the bulk of the writing, remember the "KISS" principle" "Keep It Simple, Stupid!"— especially if you are a lawyer. Use simple, clear language, not legalisms. Writing the legal lingo is what you'll pay the lawyer to do, after you and the other family members have worked out the details. It's not easy to write things simply and explicitly, so you might read parts to other members, solely for commentary of style and clarity. In fact, English Professor Ken recommends that you always read aloud whatever you write. The ear is one of the best writing tools you have, and it is usually underutilized.

If you find that certain family members are particularly difficult, resisting compromise or consensus, it's very important for you to avoid the temptation to say, "That mule-headed @#$%^&* is just a pain in the @#$%^&* and if he won't agree, he can just forget about being part of this family!" Or words to that effect. What could be happening may not be merely the result of congenital cantankerousness, but of truly different world views because of generational or regional differences. Each of the authors is very much aware of how differently our respective offspring perceive things, not just our summer house or the family, but the world in general. They have different ideas of what makes people tick, and these are going to lead to different opinions about the ways to use and maintain our summer house.

Judy has also discovered striking regional differences in attitudes and practices with summer houses. Trying not to show any bias (so please don't write and complain if you disagree with the following), she has found that families with summer houses in the Northeast tend to be more individualistic, protective of individual nuclear family prerogatives, and may want things spelled out in detail. There is also a strong "Puritan Ethic" of work before play, of putting time and effort into the work year and into the summer house before one kicks back and relaxes, related to the need to spell out responsibilities that all are to assume in turn.

In contrast, Midwestern and Western families tend to be more "laid back" about details, may think more in terms of the extended family, grandparents, aunts, uncles, cousins, etc., than the individual nuclear family of Mom, Dad and the children. They are also likely to be more relaxed about the Puritan Ethic. So if you are a New Englander dealing with a Midwestern cousin, your differences may derive more from regional culture than individual idiosyncrasies. Such differences can be overcome if the individuals show respect for each other and really try to understand what lies behind their insistence that décor decisions be spelled out or that they not be spelled out. Again, what is important is what is best for the entire family.

When you have wrangled all the details and have a completed agreement, then you can go to the lawyer. Make sure that he or she knows what the fee is for, to make legal all you have worked out, not to critique and suggest amendments to your agreement. Some might ask why it is necessary to legalize everything, once you have achieved consensus. The simple answer is that ownership, taxes, liability, inheritance, and so on, are legal matters. They can't be handled by a consensus.

In a larger sense, the legality of the agreement will give it authority and force through succeeding generations. Thirty years from now, your children are less likely to say, "Well, that's what they all wanted back then. There's no reason we have to live by their ideas."

You might look at your formal agreement as your Family Constitution. It spells out a number of policies and procedures for using the summer house. It may be amended, but not without a lot of careful thought, discussion and agreement by more than the simple majority of family members. More importantly, the principles that underlie it will guide your descendants in the myriad small ways they use the summer house and interact with each other. Respect for the property and for each other, cooperation in working for the good of all, and yes, even love are more likely to be the obvious features of the family with a good formal agreement guiding the use of their summer house.

WHAT NOW?

Do your homework. Talk, write, email, send carrier pigeons to any and all family members with some interest or legal claim on the summer house. Set up sub-committees among like-minded or same-generation kinfolk, to become engaged in the process of figuring out the best possible agreement under the circumstances, by doing some of the work. Keep an open mind. And never forget that the ultimate purpose is family leisure and enjoyment of the place, and of each other enjoying the place. If you lose sight of that, you have lost the site, as well.

If you want more background information but aren't sure about getting Judy's book, check its table of contents, reprinted on the next page. An order form follows. Use the order form if you or family members want copies of this book, or hers -- and let your bookstore know how to reach us, as well. If you tear it out and then misplace it, here are the various ways you can get in touch with us:

Ken Huggins
716:482-1899
huggins@MCCVM.IS.MONROECC.EDU

Judy Balfe
973: 746-4851
Jbalfe@home.com

and to order more copies of either or both books, by VISA or MasterCard:
1-877-PASSTON (1-877-727-7866)
or checks made out to: *Passing It On*
and mailed to: Heartland Distributors
RR 2 Box 189B
Susquehanna, PA 18847
or check out our website: www.PassingItOn.com

PASSING IT ON:
THE INHERITANCE AND USE OF SUMMER HOUSES
and
HOW TO PASS IT ON:
THE OWNERSHIP AND USE OF SUMMER HOUSES

ORDER FORM

Please detach at left and enclose with your check, as follows:

Single Copy Orders:

Passing It On: The Inheritance and Use of Summer Houses

@ $22.50 per copy + $3.50 shipping & handling ________

How to Pass It On: The Ownership and Use of Summer Houses

@ 7.50 per copy + $2.00 shipping & handling ________

Both Books Together

@ 25.00 + $4.00 shipping & handling 29 –

I would like to order _____ Copies of ***Passing It On***

_____ Copies of ***How to Pass It On***

1 Sets of both books

Total amount for books: 25 –

Total shipping & handling 4 –

Total 29 –

For bulk orders, VISA or MasterCard orders, or other information, call toll free:

1-877-PASSTON (1-877-727-7866)

Or lws@epix.net

Or check our website: www.PassingItOn.com for further information

Please send to the following address:

Name______________________________

Affiliation or Business (if applicable)______________________

Street, Apartment number etc:______________________

City, State, Zip: ______________________

A CHECK FOR THE FULL AMOUNT MUST ACCOMPANY YOUR ORDER

made out to: ***PASSING IT ON***

and mailed to: Heartland Distributors

RR2 Box 189B

Susquehanna, PA 18847

PASSING IT ON: THE INHERITANCE AND USE OF SUMMER HOUSES

Judith Huggins Balfe

CONTENTS